Why Bears Have Short Tails

Retold by Elsie Nelley
Illustrations by Dale Newman

One cold day in winter,
Fox saw two men
sitting by a barrow.

The barrow was filled
with fish.
The men were not looking
at Fox.

So Fox came up behind them
and took some of their fish.

Bear came out of the forest.
He saw Fox eating the fish.

Bear got a surprise.

"Where did you catch
your fish?" he said.
"There is thick ice
all over the river."

Now, Fox liked to play tricks
on Bear, so he said,
"If you meet me here
in the morning,
I will show you
a secret place."

"I will be here," said Bear.

The next day,

Fox took Bear along a path,

behind some rocks,

and down to the river.

"Sit down by that hole

over there in the ice,"

said Fox.

Bear sat down by the hole.

"Now, push your tail
down the hole
and into the water," said Fox.
"Stay very still.
Fish will bite your tail.
Then you can pull your tail
out of the water
and catch them."

Bear sat and sat
on the ice.

He called out to Fox,
"Is it time to pull my tail
out of the water?"

"No, not yet," said Fox.
"Don't move or the fish
will swim away."

The next time Bear called out,
Fox had gone.

"Good," said Bear.
"I will pull my tail
out of this hole to see
if I have some fish on it."

Bear pulled and pulled
and **pulled**!
But his tail was stuck
in the ice.

Bear pulled so hard
that his beautiful long tail
broke off.

And that is why bears
have short tails.